MW00534485

DEVOTION

Hymns of Faith, Hope, and Love for Solo Piano

Jay Rouse

Editor: Lloyd Larson
Music Engraving: MacMusic, Inc.
Cover Design: Patti Jeffers

ISBN: 978-0-7877-6323-7

lillenas
PUBLISHING COMPANY
www.lorenz.com

Foreword

My piano at home is in the living room with a big window that looks out onto the woods behind our house. It's one of the most peaceful places in our home and I can't count the number of times I've sat there playing, looking out that window watching it rain or snow, seeing the sun come up, or watching the wind in the trees. It has always been a special place for me and I have many memories of worship there; times of devotion at the piano in that space.

When this book idea was presented to me, I was immediately drawn to it. These are all favorite hymns of mine; songs that have ministered to me through the years. I approached each arrangement with ministry in mind and, because the words of these hymns are so meaningful, I kept the lyrics on the piano as I wrote. While the title **Devotion** kind of sets a meditative tone for the book, I tried to visit several different styles and I think the arrangements here can fit into many different settings and be encouraging to you and those you'll be ministering to as you play.

The sub-title for this book is: *Hymns of Faith, Hope, and Love for Solo Piano.* I can't read that without thinking of 1 Corinthians 13: *And now these three remain: faith, hope, and love. But the greatest of these is love.* I pray my life is marked by these traits. I pray my music encourages faith, hope, and love. And my prayer for you is that these arrangements will be meaningful for you whether you're playing at church or sitting at your piano, in your living room.

Blessings!

– Jay Rouse

About the Arranger

Watch Jay Rouse sit at a piano and a few things are immediately evident. There's the thoughtful way he has of capturing and engaging his listeners, the deep personal artistry, the talent and the gifting. But if you stop there, you will have missed it. There is another desire that drives his passion to play and to create; to understand not just notes, but also the spaces between the notes. That desire is worship. Jay Rouse is a worshiper and the piano and the music are the creative vehicle he uses to facilitate the worship. Ask him about what he is most passionate and he will say, "…having the opportunity to lead people in worship and better understand who they are in Christ."

Jay's talents and ministry have taken him into countless venues, working with a wide range of artists. He has toured extensively in the USA and abroad with Sandi Patty as her Music Director and accompanist, recorded her American Songbook project in London, traveled to Japan and Korea, and more recently to Carnegie Hall. Additionally, he has worked with Christian artists Bill and Gloria Gaither, the Gaither Vocal Band, Kathy Trocolli, Buddy Greene, and Veritas.

Jay Rouse is the chief Creative Director for PraiseGathering Music Group, composing some of the top-selling choral anthems in Christian music. He is one of the leading arrangers, orchestrators, and producers in the industry. He continues to oversee the creative development of new publications for PraiseGathering Music Group and Gaither Music Company as well as many other leading choral print publishers. All of this has created a body of work that comprises more than three hundred octavos and over fifty best-selling choral musicals. As a keyboard artist and arranger, Jay has sixteen books and CDs in print.

Born and raised in Florida, the Gulf coast with its ocean waves and salt breezes is the place Jay likes best to recharge and restore, the place that always feels like home. When he's not working, you might find Jay there with his family, reading a good book, and drinking sweet tea with lime. Throw in some good barbeque, maybe a slice of key lime pie or carrot cake for dessert, and that's all it will take. Jay and Amy live in Anderson, Indiana. They are the parents of two children, Thatcher and Londyn.

Contents

I. Faith

II. Hope

III. Love

763237-3

I. FAITH
My Faith Has Found a Resting Place

Norwegian Folk Melody
Arr. by Jay Rouse

Thoughtfully ♩ = ca. 63

Do Not
Photocopy

Slightly faster ♩ = ca. 69

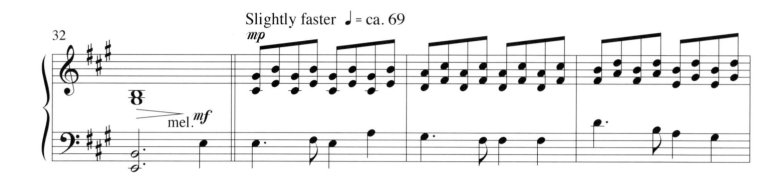

mel.

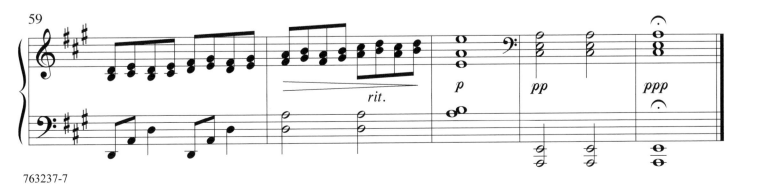

A Mighty Fortress Is Our God

With freedom ♩ = 108-112

MARTIN LUTHER
Arr. by Jay Rouse

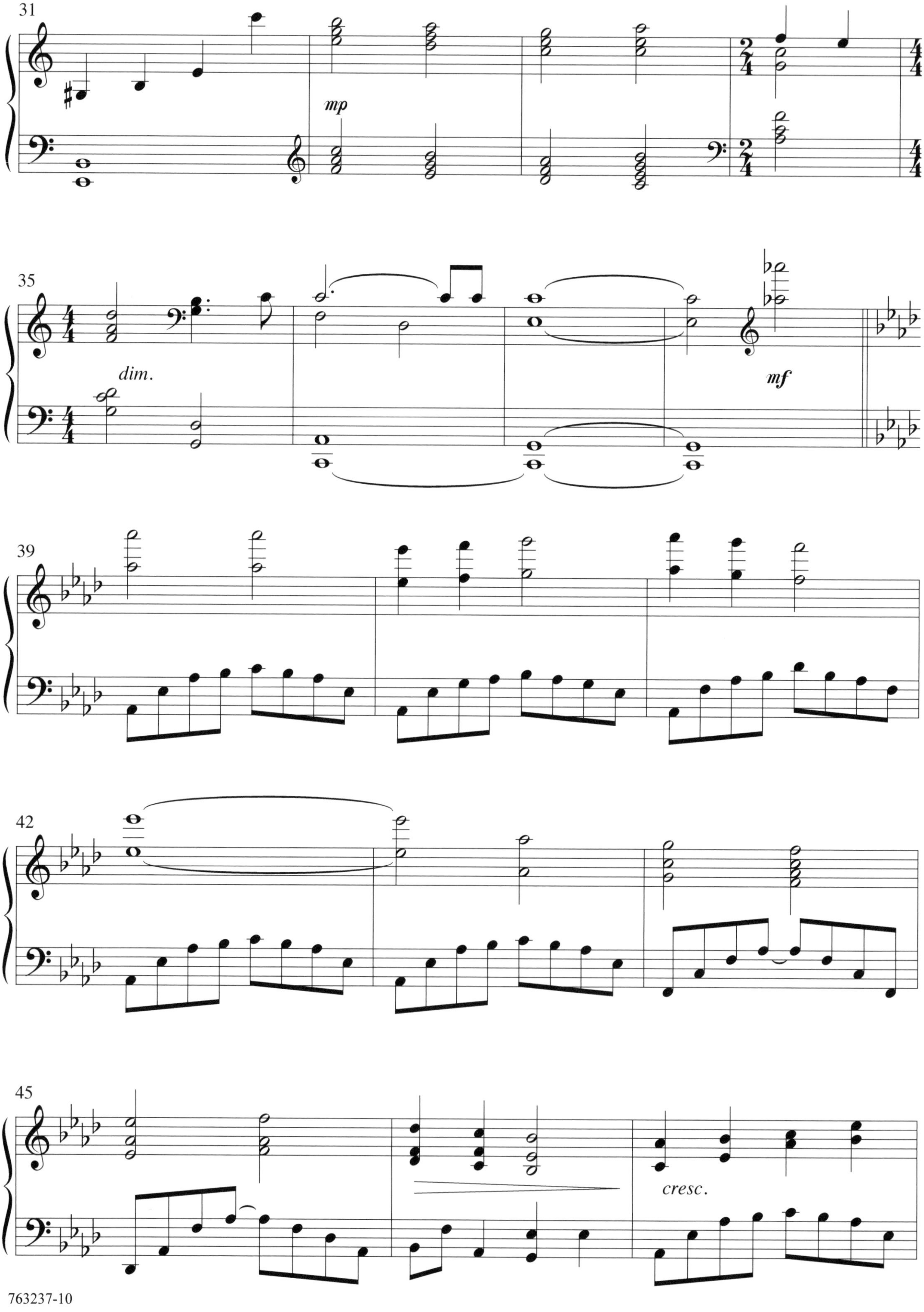
31
mp
35
dim.
mf
39
42
45
cresc.

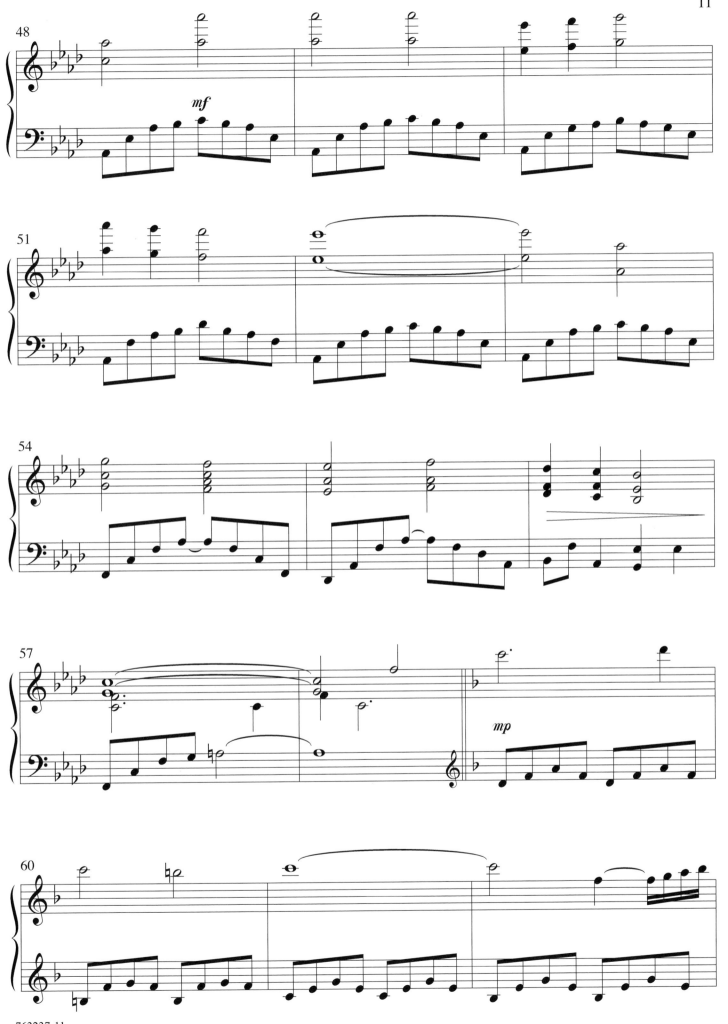

12

763237-12

Day by Day

OSCAR AHNFELT
Arr. by Jay Rouse

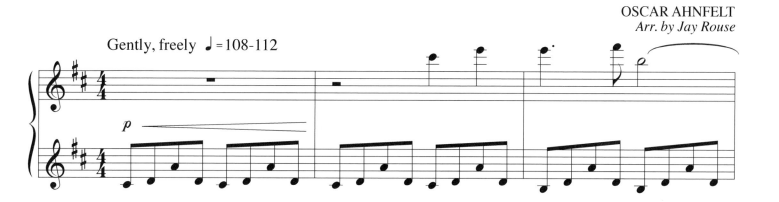

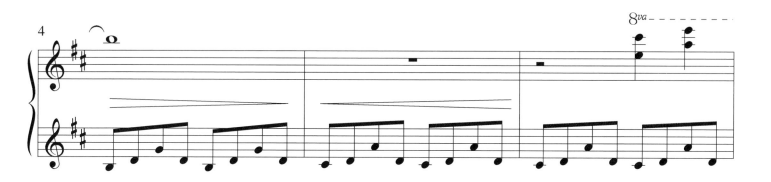

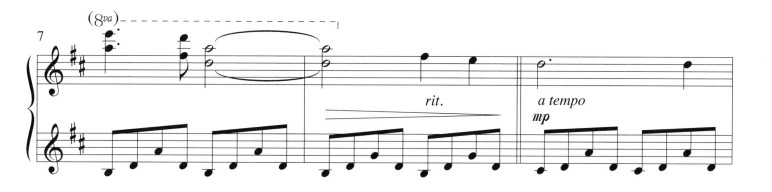

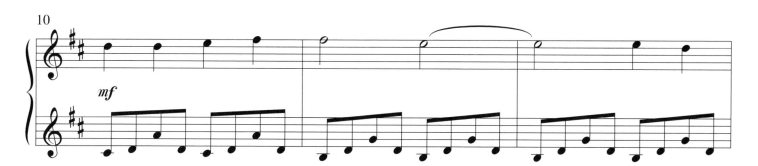

II. HOPE
O God, Our Help in Ages Past

WILLIAM CROFT
Arr. by Jay Rouse

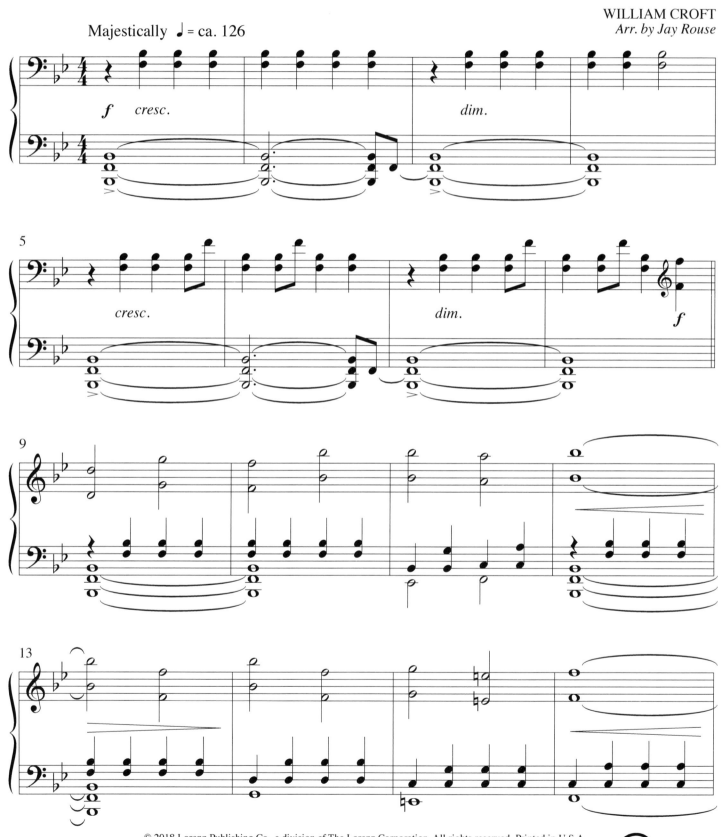

Give Me Jesus

African American Spiritual
Arr. by Jay Rouse

Slowly, freely ♩ = ca. 88

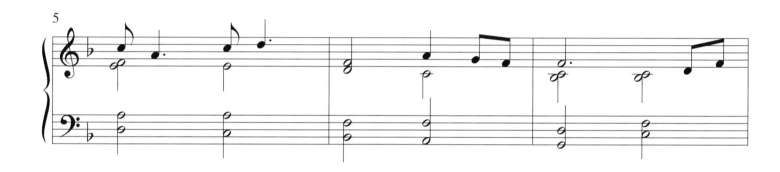

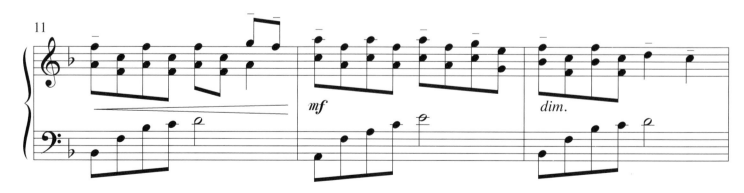

It Is Well with My Soul

PHILIP P. BLISS
Arr. by Jay Rouse

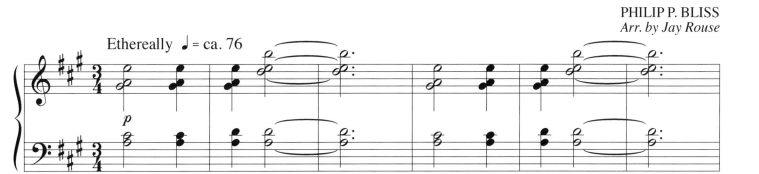

Do Not
Photocopy

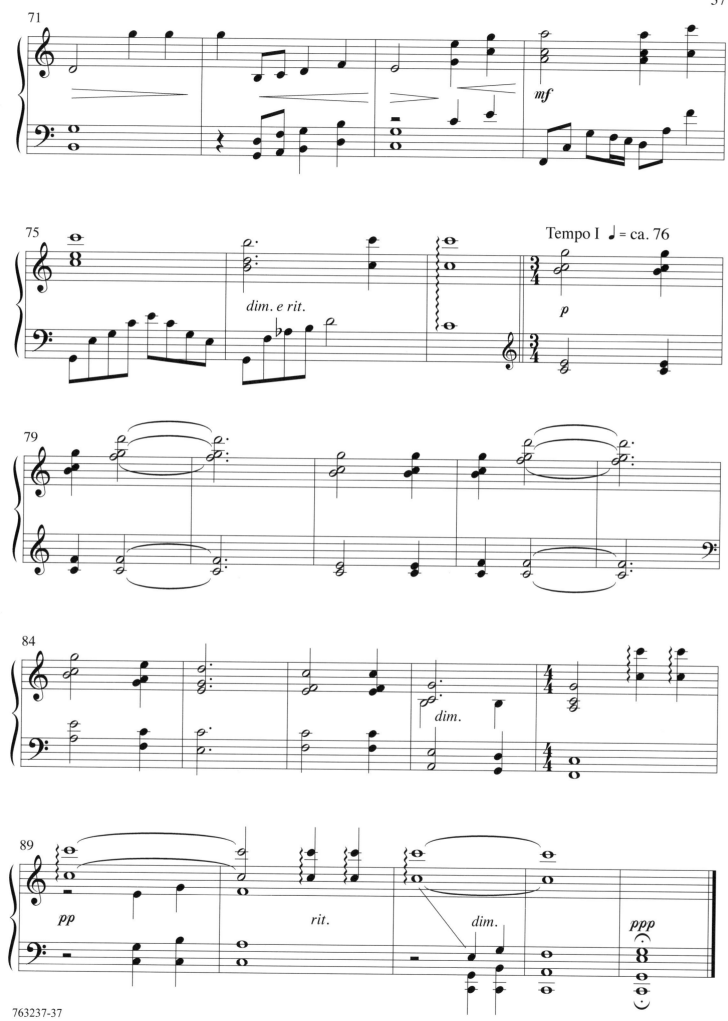

I Am Thine, O Lord

WILLIAM H. DOANE
Arr. by Jay Rouse

763237-38

42

III. LOVE
O Love That Will Not Let Me Go

ALBERT L. PEACE
Arr. by Jay Rouse

Tenderly, freely ♩ = 96-100

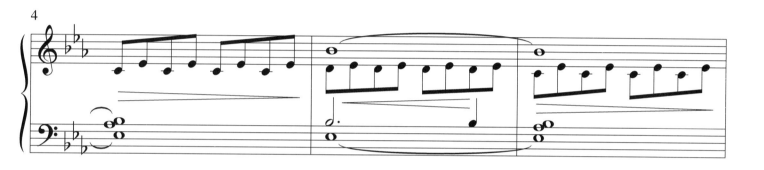

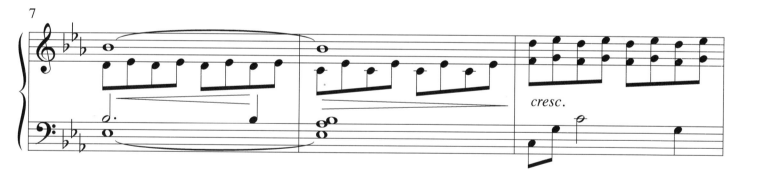

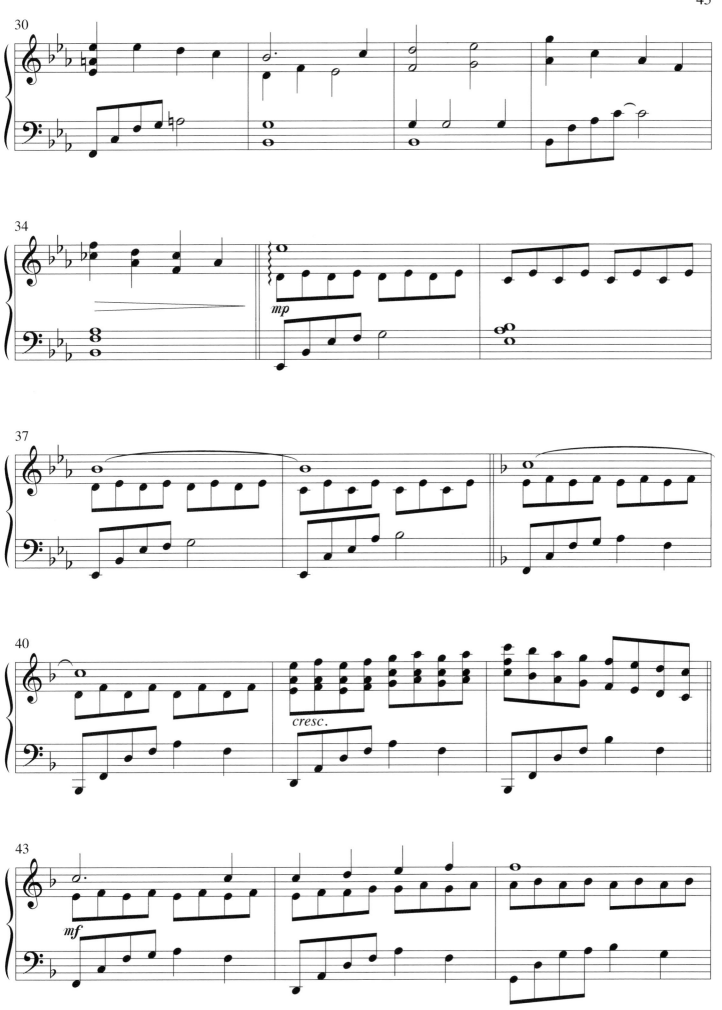

Love Divine, All Loves Excelling

JOHN ZUNDEL
Arr. by Jay Rouse

Steadily ♩ = ca. 116

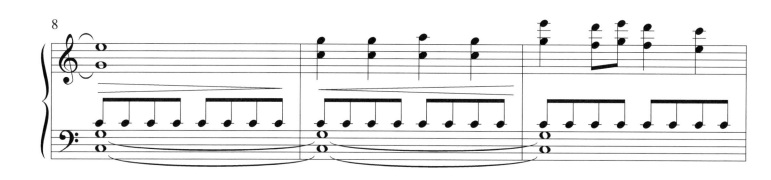

763237-48

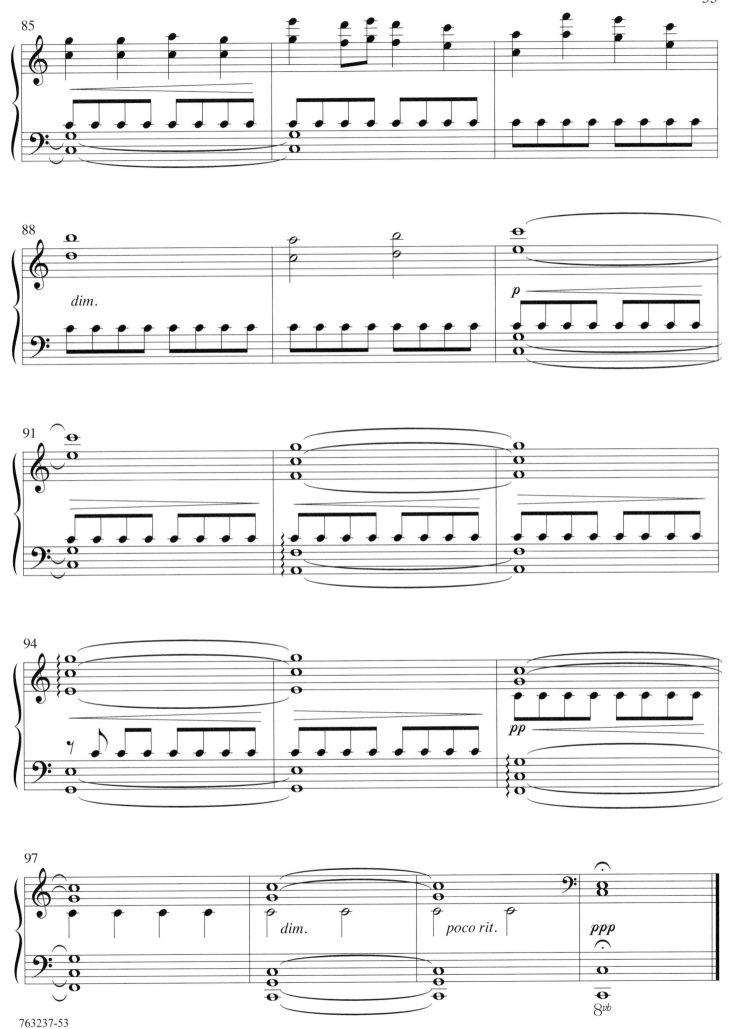

My Jesus, I Love Thee

ADONIRAM J. GORDON
Arr. by Jay Rouse

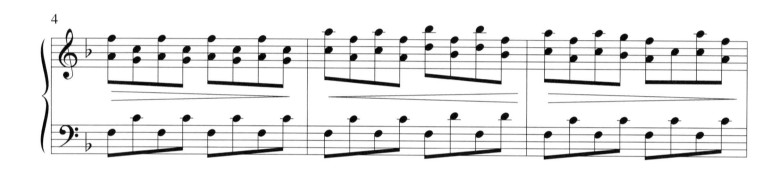

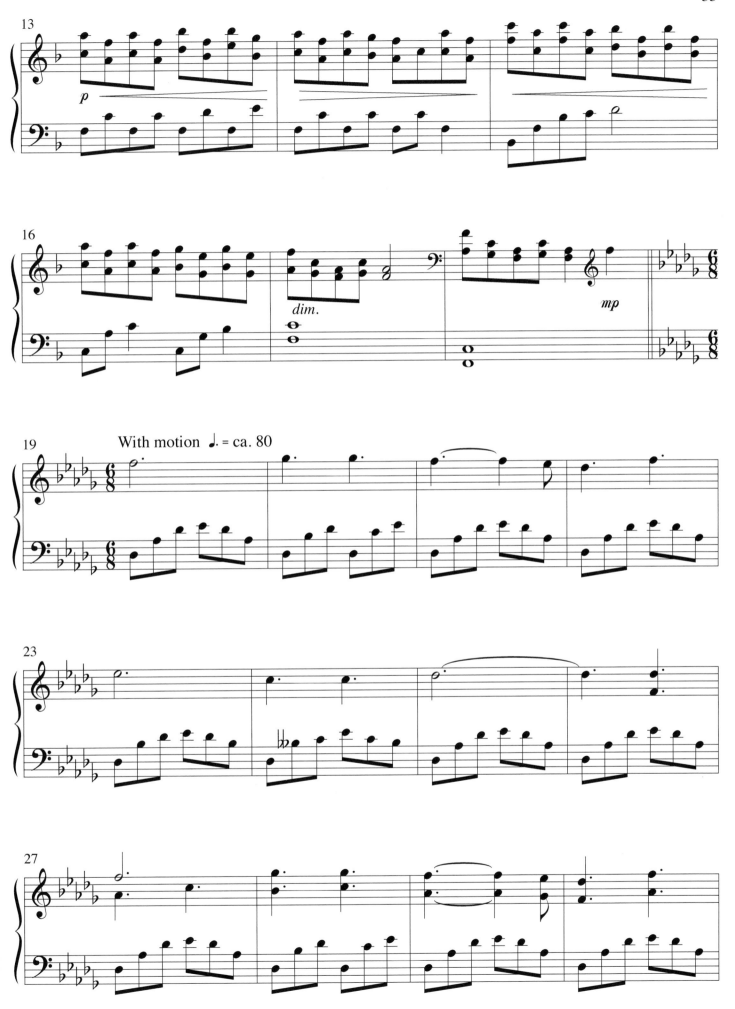

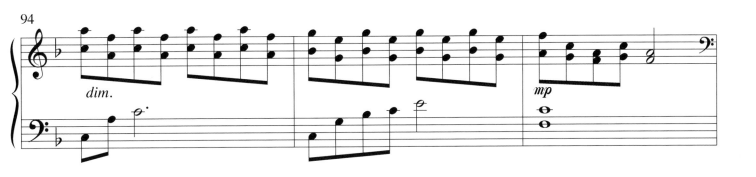